# STEP-BY-STEP

# Pizzas

# Pizzas

WENDY LEE

||| •PARRAGON• |||

First published in Great Britain in 1994 by
Parragon Book Service Ltd
Unit 13-17
Avonbridge Trading Estate
Atlantic Road
Avonmouth
Bristol BS11 9QD

ISBN 1 85813 884 1

Produced by Haldane Mason, London
Printed in Italy


*Acknowledgements*
*Art Direction:* Ron Samuels
*Editor:* Joanna Swinnerton
*Series design:* Pedro & Frances Pra-Lopez/Kingfisher Design
*Page design:* F14 Creative Consultants Ltd
*Photography:* Joff Lee
*Styling:* John Lee Studios
*Home Economist:* Wendy Lee


Photographs on pages 6, 18, 34, 50 and 64 reproduced by permission of ZEFA Picture Library UK Ltd.

Note
*Unless otherwise stated, milk is assumed to be full-fat, eggs are standard size 2 and pepper is freshly ground black pepper.*

# Contents

# CHAPTER ONE

# *Basics*

The success of a pizza depends on the quality of the bread dough base and the tomato sauce. A homemade bread dough base topped with a delicious freshly made tomato sauce will give you the closest thing possible to an authentic Italian pizza in your own kitchen.

If time is short and you cannot wait for the dough to rise, make either a scone (biscuit) or a potato base. Alternatively, ready-made bases or pizza-base mixes can suffice, but these do not provide the same aroma of home-cooked bread, nor the sense of achievement.

Choose tomatoes that are canned in juice rather than water, as these make a thicker sauce. Many brands of chopped tomato have added ingredients such as garlic, chilli, onion, basil and mixed herbs, which will add extra flavour to your tomato sauces.

For pizza fans and busy cooks, make double the quantity of the basic bread dough and freeze the dough that is not required after it has been kneaded. Or you can roll out the dough in the usual way, arrange the topping on it, bake for 10 minutes, then cool and freeze. Reheat by cooking from frozen for 15 minutes. The tomato sauces also freeze well, so make up large quantities and freeze the excess, and then you can have pizzas whenever you wish.

Opposite: *The many-levelled red tile roofs and deep green trees of a typical Italian hill town.*

**STEP 3**

**STEP 4**

**STEP 5**

**STEP 6**

# BREAD DOUGH BASE

*Traditionally, pizza bases are made from bread dough; this recipe will give you a base similar to an Italian pizza. Always use ordinary plain flour which can be white, wholemeal or a combination of both.*

MAKES ONE 25 CM/10 IN ROUND

15 g/¹/₂ oz fresh yeast or 1 tsp dried or easy-
    blend yeast
90 ml/ 3¹/₂ fl oz tepid water
¹/₂ tsp sugar
1 tbsp olive oil
175 g/6 oz plain flour
1 tsp salt

**1** Combine the fresh yeast with the water and sugar in a bowl. If using dried yeast, sprinkle it over the surface of the water and whisk in until dissolved.

**2** Leave the mixture to rest in a warm place for 10–15 minutes until frothy on the surface. Stir in the olive oil.

**3** Sift the flour and salt into a large bowl. If using easy-blend yeast, stir it in at this point. Make a well in the centre and pour in the yeast liquid, or water and oil (without the sugar for easy-blend yeast).

**4** Using either floured hands or a wooden spoon, mix together to form a dough. Turn out on to a floured work surface and knead for about 5 minutes until smooth and elastic.

**5** Place in a large greased plastic bag and leave in a warm place for about 1 hour or until doubled in size. Airing cupboards are often the best places for this, as the temperature remains constant.

**6** Turn out on to a lightly floured work surface and 'knock back' by punching the dough. This releases any air bubbles which would make the pizza uneven. Knead 4 or 5 times. The dough is now ready to use.

### USING YEAST

Many people may be nervous about using yeast, but it is really quite simple, especially if you use an easy-blend variety. See page 77 for tips on cooking with yeast.

### FREEZING

Pizza dough can be frozen after the first kneading. Wrap in clingfilm and label with the date and quantity before freezing. Defrost at room temperature and leave to rise in the usual way. Continue as from step 5.

STEP 2

STEP 3

STEP 4

STEP 5

# SCONE (BISCUIT) BASE

*This is a quick and easy alternative to the bread dough base. If you do not have time to wait for bread dough to rise, a scone (biscuit) base is the next best thing.*

MAKES ONE 25 CM/10 IN ROUND

*175 g/6 oz self-raising flour*
*¹/₂ tsp salt*
*30 g/1 oz butter*
*120 ml/4 fl oz milk*

**1** Sift the flour and salt into a bowl.

**2** Rub in the butter with your fingertips until it resembles fine breadcrumbs.

**3** Make a well in the centre of the flour and butter mixture and pour in nearly all the milk at once. Mix in quickly with a knife. Add the remaining milk only if necessary to mix to a soft dough.

**4** Turn the dough out on to a floured work surface and knead by turning and pressing with the heel of your hand 3 or 4 times.

**5** Either roll out or press the dough into a 25 cm/10 in circle on a lightly greased baking sheet or pizza pan. Push up the edge all round slightly to form a ridge and use immediately.

## ADDING TASTE

You can vary the taste of your scone (biscuit) base by adding a little grated cheese or ½ teaspoon dried oregano or mixed herbs to it for a more interesting flavour. Add your extra flavourings to the mixture after rubbing in the butter.

## RUBBING IN

When rubbing in butter, it helps if your hands and the butter are very cold. Cut the butter into small dice first, then cut it into the flour with two knives held like scissors. Finally, rub in the remaining lumps of butter with your fingertips, remembering to keep your hands cool as you go.

STEP 1

STEP 2

STEP 3

STEP 4

# POTATO BASE

*This is an unusual pizza base made from mashed potatoes and flour and is a great way to use up any leftover boiled potatoes. Children love this base and you will soon have them asking for more.*

MAKES ONE 25 CM/10 IN ROUND

*250 g/8 oz boiled potatoes*
*60 g/2 oz butter or margarine*
*125 g/4 oz self-raising flour*
*¹/₂ tsp salt*

**1** If the potatoes are hot, mash them, then stir in the butter until it has melted and is distributed evenly throughout the potatoes. Leave to cool.

**2** Sift the flour and salt together and stir into the mashed potato to form a soft dough.

**3** If the potatoes are cold, mash them without adding the butter. Sift the flour and salt into a bowl. Rub in the butter with your fingertips until the mixture resembles fine breadcrumbs, then stir the flour and butter mixture into the mashed potatoes to form a soft dough.

**4** Either roll out or press the dough into a 25 cm/10 in circle on a lightly greased baking sheet or pizza pan, pushing up the edge all round slightly to form a ridge before adding the topping. This base is tricky to lift before it is cooked, so you will find it easier to handle if you roll it out directly on the baking sheet.

**5** If the base is not required for cooking immediately, you can cover it with clingfilm (plastic wrap) and chill it for up to 2 hours.

## USING INSTANT COOKED POTATO

If time is short and you do not have any leftover cooked potato, make up a batch of instant dried mashed potato, keeping the consistency fairly dry, and use that instead — it will work just as well.

## EXTRA FLAVOUR

To add more flavour to this base, you can try adding some dried or fresh herbs, fried chopped onion, grated cheese or even a grated carrot. Any of these will add a delicious subtle taste to your pizza base.

# TOMATO SAUCE

*Use cans of either chopped or whole plum tomatoes for this sauce.*
*I prefer to use chopped tomatoes as it saves time, and the plum tomatoes*
*tend to be on the watery side. For a really spicy sauce, add a chopped*
*fresh red chilli when frying the onions.*

STEP 1

MAKES ENOUGH TO COVER ONE
25 CM/10 IN PIZZA BASE

*1 small onion, chopped*
*1 garlic clove, crushed*
*1 tbsp olive oil*
*220 g/7 oz can chopped tomatoes*
*2 tsp tomato purée*
*½ tsp sugar*
*½ tsp dried oregano*
*1 bay leaf*
*salt and pepper*

STEP 2

**1** Fry the onion and garlic gently in the oil for 5 minutes until softened but not browned.

**2** Add the tomatoes, tomato purée, sugar, oregano, bay leaf and seasoning. Stir well.

**3** Bring to the boil, cover and simmer gently for 20 minutes, stirring occasionally, until you have a thickish sauce.

**4** Remove the bay leaf and adjust the seasoning to taste. Leave to cool completely before using. This sauce keeps well in a screw-top jar in the refrigerator for up to 1 week.

### TOMATOES

Tomatoes are actually berries and are related to potatoes. There are many different shapes and sizes of this versatile fruit. The one most used in Italian cooking is the plum tomato. Large beefsteak tomatoes or small, sweet cherry tomatoes are ideal for use in accompanying salads.

### USING CHILLIES

Take care when chopping chillies as they can burn your skin. Handle them as little as possible – you could even wear rubber gloves if you wish. Always wash your hands thoroughly afterwards, and don't touch your face or eyes before you have washed your hands.

Remove chilli seeds before chopping the chillies, as they are the hottest part, and shouldn't be allowed to slip into the

STEP 3

STEP 4

STEP 1

STEP 2

STEP 3

STEP 3

# SPECIAL TOMATO SAUCE

*This sauce is made with fresh tomatoes. Use the plum variety whenever available and always choose the reddest tomatoes to give a better colour and sweetness to the sauce. When plum tomatoes are readily available, make several batches of sauce and freeze them.*

MAKES ENOUGH TO COVER ONE
25 CM/10 IN PIZZA BASE.

1 small onion, chopped
1 small red (bell) pepper, chopped
1 garlic clove, crushed
2 tbsp olive oil
250 g/8 oz tomatoes
1 tbsp tomato purée
1 tsp soft brown sugar
2 tsp chopped fresh basil
$^1/_2$ tsp dried oregano
1 bay leaf
salt and pepper

**1** Fry the onion, (bell) pepper and garlic gently in the oil for 5 minutes until softened but not browned.

**2** Cut a cross in the base of each tomato and place them in a bowl. Pour on boiling water and leave for about 45 seconds. Drain, and then plunge in cold water. The skins will slide off easily.

**3** Chop the tomatoes, discarding any hard cores. Add the chopped tomatoes, tomato purée, sugar, herbs and seasoning to the onion mixture. Stir well. Bring to the boil, cover and simmer gently for 30 minutes, stirring occasionally, until you have a thickish sauce.

**4** Remove the bay leaf and adjust the seasoning to taste. Leave to cool completely before using.

**5** This sauce will keep well in a screw-top jar in the refrigerator for up to a week.

### SKINNING TOMATOES

You can skin tomatoes in another way if you have a gas stove. Cut a cross in the base of the tomato, push it on to a fork and hold it over a gas flame, turning it slowly so that the skin heats evenly all over. The skin will start to bubble and split, and should then slide off easily.

# *Meat & Fish Pizzas*

A meat or fish pizza provides a very substantial, well-balanced meal. Pizzas can be topped with almost any type of meat or fish, which can lead to many highly imaginative dishes.

As pizzas are baked in a hot oven for a fairly short time, the meat should be cooked before it is added to the pizza, or it will end up undercooked. For the best results the meat should be minced (ground) or cut into small pieces. Bacon can be added in its raw state as this is usually thinly sliced and cooks very quickly.

There are almost endless varieties of salamis, sliced cured meats, hams, sausages and bacon, either pre-packaged or from the delicatessen counter, which make perfect pizza toppings.

Canned or fresh fish or shellfish are wonderful on pizzas. Use anything from whitebait, mussels or clams in their shells, canned sardines and monkfish to just plain cod. The most popular fish known to the pizza are, of course, anchovies and you either love them or hate them. One of the most famous pizzas on which they are used is the Pizza Napoletana, which originated in Naples; the topping is basically anchovies and olives without any cheese. If you find anchovies too salty, it helps to soak them in a little milk before using.

Opposite: *Sunset over the Grand Canal, Venice.*

STEP 1

STEP 3

STEP 4

STEP 6

# CHICKEN SATAY

*Satays are usually served with peanut sauces, so this pizza is topped with chicken which has been marinated in a peanut sauce. For an even simpler version, you could use just the crunchy peanut butter.*

SERVES 2–4

2 tbsp crunchy peanut butter
1 tbsp lime juice
1 tbsp soy sauce
3 tbsp milk
1 red chilli, deseeded and chopped
1 garlic clove, crushed
175 g/6 oz cooked chicken, diced
1 quantity Bread Dough Base (see page 8)
1 quantity Special Tomato Sauce (see page 16)
4 spring onions (scallions), trimmed and chopped
60 g/2 oz Mozzarella cheese, grated
olive oil for drizzling
salt and pepper

**1** Mix together the peanut butter, lime juice, soy sauce, milk, chilli and garlic in a bowl to form a sauce. Season well.

**2** Add the chicken to the peanut sauce and stir until well coated. Cover and leave to marinate in a cool place for about 20 minutes.

**3** Roll out or press the dough, using a rolling pin or your hands, into a 25 cm/10 in circle on a lightly floured work surface. Place on a large greased baking sheet or pizza pan and push up the edge a little. Cover and leave to rise slightly for 10 minutes in a warm place.

**4** When the dough has risen, spread with the tomato sauce almost to the edge.

**5** Top with the spring onions (scallions) and chicken pieces, spooning over the peanut sauce.

**6** Sprinkle over the cheese. Drizzle with a little olive oil and season well. Bake in a preheated oven at 200°C/400°F/Gas Mark 6, for 18–20 minutes, or until the crust is golden. Serve immediately with a simple vegetable stir-fry.

### TIMESAVERS

If you are short of time, buy ready-cooked chicken, remove any skin and cut it into chunks. You can save more time by using crunchy peanut butter instead of making the satay sauce.

STEP 2

STEP 3

STEP 4

STEP 5

# AMERICAN HOT CHILLI BEEF

*This deep-pan pizza is topped with minced (ground) beef, red kidney beans and jalapeño chillies, which are small, green and very hot. Add more or less chilli powder depending on personal taste. Monterey Jack is an American cheese; if it is unavailable, use a mature Cheddar instead.*

SERVES 2–4

FOR THE DOUGH BASE:
20 g/³/₄ oz fresh yeast or 1¹/₂ tsp dried or
    easy-blend yeast
125 ml/4 fl oz tepid water
1 tsp sugar
3 tbsp olive oil
250 g/8 oz plain flour
1 tsp salt

FOR THE TOPPING:
1 small onion, sliced thinly
1 garlic clove, crushed
¹/₂ yellow (bell) pepper, chopped
1 tbsp olive oil
175 g/6 oz lean minced (ground) beef
¹/₄ tsp chilli powder
¹/₄ tsp ground cumin
220 g/7 oz can red kidney beans, drained
1 quantity Tomato Sauce (see page 15)
30 g/1 oz jalapeño chillies, sliced
60 g/2 oz Mozzarella cheese, sliced thinly
60 g/2 oz Monterey Jack cheese, grated
olive oil for drizzling
salt and pepper
chopped parsley to garnish

**1** For the deep-pan dough base, use the same method as the Bread Dough Base recipe (see page 8).

**2** Roll out or press the dough, using a rolling pin or your hands, into a 23 cm/9 in circle on a lightly floured work surface. Place on a pizza pan and push up the edge to fit and form a small ridge. Cover and leave to rise slightly for about 10 minutes.

**3** Fry the onion, garlic and (bell) pepper gently in the oil for 5 minutes until softened but not browned. Increase the heat slightly and add the beef, chilli and cumin. Fry for 5 minutes, stirring occasionally. Remove from the heat and stir in the kidney beans. Season well.

**4** Spread the tomato sauce over the dough almost to the edge and top with the meat mixture.

**5** Top with the sliced chillies and Mozzarella cheese and sprinkle over the grated cheese. Drizzle with a little olive oil and season.

**6** Bake in a preheated oven at 200°C/400°F/Gas Mark 6 for 18–20 minutes, or until the crust is golden. Serve immediately sprinkled with chopped parsley.

# AUBERGINE (EGGPLANT) AND LAMB

*An unusual fragrant, spiced pizza topped with minced (ground) lamb and aubergine (eggplant) on a bread base. Pimientos are skinned, sweet, elongated red (bell) peppers, which are available canned in oil or brine; if these are unavailable, use sliced red (bell) pepper instead.*

STEP 1

SERVES 2–4

1 small aubergine (eggplant), diced
1 quantity Bread Dough Base (see page 8)
1 small onion, sliced thinly
1 garlic clove, crushed
1 tsp cumin seeds
1 tbsp olive oil
175 g/6 oz minced (ground) lamb
30 g/1 oz pimiento, sliced thinly
2 tbsp chopped fresh coriander (cilantro)
1 quantity Special Tomato Sauce (see page 16)
90 g/3 oz Mozzarella cheese, sliced thinly
olive oil for drizzling
salt and pepper

**1** Sprinkle the diced aubergine (eggplant) with salt in a colander and let the bitter juices drain over a sink for about 20 minutes; then rinse and pat dry with paper towels.

**2** Roll out or press the dough, using a rolling pin or your hands, into a 25 cm/10 in circle on a lightly floured work surface. Place on a large greased baking sheet or pizza pan and push up the edge a little to form a rim.

**3** Cover and leave to rise slightly for 10 minutes in a warm place.

**4** Fry the onion, garlic and cumin seeds gently in the oil for 3 minutes. Increase the heat slightly and add the lamb, aubergine (eggplant) and pimiento. Fry for 5 minutes, stirring occasionally. Add the coriander (cilantro) and season well.

**5** Spread the tomato sauce over the dough base almost to the edge. Top with the lamb mixture.

**6** Arrange the Mozzarella slices on top. Drizzle over a little olive oil and season.

**7** Bake in a preheated oven at 200°C/400°F/Gas Mark 6 for 18–20 minutes, until the crust is crisp and golden. Serve immediately.

STEP 2

## CORIANDER (CILANTRO)

If fresh coriander (cilantro) is unavailable, substitute 1 tsp ground coriander and add 1 tbsp chopped fresh parsley for colour.

STEP 4

STEP 6

STEP 1

STEP 2

STEP 3

STEP 4

# SMOKY BACON AND PEPPERONI

*This more traditional kind of pizza is topped with pepperoni, smoked bacon and (bell) peppers covered in a smoked cheese.*

SERVES 2–4

1 quantity Bread Dough Base (see page 8)
1 tbsp olive oil
1 tbsp grated fresh Parmesan cheese
1 quantity Tomato Sauce (see page 15)
125 g/4 oz lightly smoked bacon, diced
1/2 green (bell) pepper, sliced thinly
1/2 yellow (bell) pepper, sliced thinly
60 g/2 oz pepperoni-style sliced spicy
    sausage
60 g/2 oz smoked Bavarian cheese, grated
1/2 tsp dried oregano
olive oil for drizzling
salt and pepper

**1** Roll out or press the dough, using a rolling pin or your hands, into a 25 cm/10 in circle on a lightly floured work surface. Place on a large greased baking sheet or pizza pan and push up the edge a little with your fingers, to form a rim.

**2** Brush the base with the olive oil and sprinkle the Parmesan cheese over it. Cover and leave to rise slightly in a warm place for about 10 minutes.

**3** Spread the tomato sauce over the base almost to the edge. Top with the bacon and (bell) peppers. Arrange the pepperoni slices over and sprinkle with the smoked cheese.

**4** Sprinkle over the oregano and drizzle with a little olive oil. Season well.

**5** Bake in a preheated oven at 200°C/400°F/Gas Mark 6 for 18–20 minutes, or until the crust is golden and crisp around the edge. Cut into wedges and serve immediately.

### SAVING TIME

Pre-packaged, thinly sliced pepperoni and diced bacon can be purchased from most supermarkets, which helps to save on preparation time.

### PEPPERONI

A spicy pepperoni-style sausage can be quite hot. If you prefer a milder taste, use slices of salami, chorizo or even sliced, cooked sausages in its place.

STEP 1

STEP 3

STEP 3

STEP 4

# FOUR SEASONS

*This is a traditional pizza on which the toppings are divided into four sections, each of which is supposed to depict a season of the year. Sliced pepperoni, salami or kabanos (a small, spicy sausage) can be used instead of the chorizo.*

SERVES 2–4

1 quantity Bread Dough Base (see page 8)
1 quantity Special Tomato Sauce (see page 16)
30 g/1 oz chorizo sausage, sliced thinly
30 g/1 oz button mushrooms, wiped and sliced thinly
45g/1½ oz artichoke hearts, sliced thinly
30 g/1 oz Mozzarella cheese, sliced thinly
3 anchovies, halved lengthways
2 tsp capers
4 pitted black olives, sliced
4 fresh basil leaves, shredded
olive oil for drizzling
salt and pepper

**1** Roll out or press the dough, using a rolling pin or your hands, into a 25 cm/10 in circle on a lightly floured work surface. Place on a large greased baking sheet or pizza pan and push up the edge a little.

**2** Cover and leave to rise slightly for 10 minutes in a warm place before spreading with tomato sauce almost to the edge.

**3** Put the sliced chorizo on 1 quarter of the pizza, the sliced mushrooms on another, the artichoke hearts on a third and the Mozzarella cheese and anchovies on the fourth.

**4** Dot the pizza with the capers, olives and basil leaves. Drizzle a little olive oil over the pizza and season. Do not put any salt on the anchovy section as the fish are very salty.

**5** Bake in a preheated oven at 200°C/ 400°F/Gas Mark 6 for 18–20 minutes, or until the crust is golden and crisp. Serve immediately.

## FISHY ALTERNATIVE

Fish-lovers could make a seafood four seasons pizza using prawns (shrimp), cockles, mussels and anchovies with one ingredient on each quarter, placed in a decorative arrangement.

**STEP 1**

**STEP 2**

**STEP 3**

**STEP 4**

# MARINARA

*This pizza is topped with frozen mixed seafood such as prawns (shrimp), mussels, cockles and squid rings. Alternatively, fresh seafood can be bought from the fresh fish counter in most supermarkets. If you prefer, you can just use peeled prawns (shrimp).*

SERVES 2–4

1 quantity Potato Base (see page 12)
1 quantity Special Tomato Sauce (see page 16)
200 g/7 oz frozen seafood cocktail, defrosted
1 tbsp capers
1 small yellow (bell) pepper, chopped
1 tbsp chopped fresh marjoram
½ tsp dried oregano
60 g/2 oz Mozzarella cheese, grated
15g/½ oz Parmesan cheese, grated
12 black olives
olive oil for drizzling
salt and pepper
sprig of fresh marjoram or oregano to garnish

**1** Roll out or press out the potato dough, using a rolling pin or your hands, into a 25 cm/10 in circle on a lightly floured work surface. Place on a large greased baking sheet or pizza pan and push up the edge a little with your fingers to form a rim.

**2** Spread with the tomato sauce almost to the edge.

**3** Arrange the seafood cocktail, capers and yellow (bell) pepper on the sauce.

**4** Sprinkle over the herbs and cheeses. Arrange the olives on top. Drizzle over a little olive oil and season well.

**5** Bake in a preheated oven at 200°C/400°F/Gas Mark 6 for 18–20 minutes until the edge of the pizza is crisp and golden.

**6** Transfer to a warmed serving plate, garnish with a sprig of marjoram or oregano and serve immediately.

## SEAFOOD TOPPING

If you prefer, you can replace any of the seafood with small pieces of monkfish, plaice, cod or slices of crabstick.

**STEP 1**

**STEP 3**

**STEP 4**

**STEP 5**

# ALASKA PIZZA

*Chunks of canned salmon top this tasty pizza. You can use either red or pink salmon. Red salmon will give a better colour and flavour but it can be expensive.*

Serves 2–4

*1 quantity Scone (Biscuit) Base (see page 10)*
*1 quantity Tomato Sauce (see page 15)*
*1 courgette (zucchini), grated*
*1 tomato, sliced thinly*
*100 g / 3½ oz can red or pink salmon*
*60 g / 2 oz button mushrooms, wiped and sliced*
*1 tbsp chopped fresh dill*
*½ tsp dried oregano*
*45 g / 1½ oz Mozzarella cheese, grated*
*olive oil for drizzling*
*salt and pepper*
*sprig of fresh dill to garnish*

**1** Roll out or press the dough, using a rolling pin or your hands, into a 25 cm / 10 in circle on a lightly floured work surface. Place on a large greased baking sheet or pizza pan and push up the edge a little with your fingers to form a rim.

**2** Spread with the tomato sauce almost to the edge.

**3** Top the tomato sauce with the grated courgette (zucchini), then lay the tomato slices on top.

**4** Drain the can of salmon. Remove any bones and skin and flake the fish. Arrange on the pizza with the mushrooms. Sprinkle over the herbs and cheese. Drizzle with a little olive oil and season well.

**5** Bake in a preheated oven at 200°C/400°F/Gas Mark 6, for 18–20 minutes, or until the edge is golden and crisp.

**6** Transfer to a warmed serving plate and serve immediately, garnished with a sprig of dill.

ECONOMY VERSION

If salmon is too pricey, use either canned tuna or sardines to make a delicious everyday fish pizza. Choose canned fish in brine for a healthier topping. If fresh dill is unavailable, you can use parsley instead.

CHAPTER THREE

# *Vegetarian Pizzas*

Although this chapter is for vegetarians, anyone can enjoy these pizzas. With a little imagination there is no end to the variety of vegetarian pizzas that can be produced, and as vegetables are so full of colour, they make attractive and tempting toppings. Choose the best quality fresh vegetables and herbs to give maximum flavour.

Tofu and quorn make very good pizza toppings and they marinate particularly well. For extra flavour use a smoked tofu. Minced (ground) quorn (a myco-protein derived from fungi) can be used in place of minced (ground) meat and will make an excellent American Hot Chilli Pizza.

A wide variety of antipasti are sold in jars of olive oil, such as artichoke hearts, sun-dried tomatoes, sliced (bell) peppers and mushrooms, which make perfect pizza topping ingredients. Use the oil in the jar to drizzle over the pizza before baking to keep it moist.

If you prefer, you can use vegetarian Cheddar or Mozzarella cheese, which are widely available. You can substitute the vegetarian variety for the cheese suggested in most of the recipes in this section (except in the Three Cheese and Artichoke recipe) for a slightly different taste.

Opposite: *The sun sets over the lush Chianti vineyards in Tuscany.*

STEP 1

STEP 3

STEP 4

STEP 5

# FLORENTINE

*A pizza adaptation of Eggs Florentine – sliced hard-boiled (hard-cooked) eggs on freshly cooked spinach with a little nutmeg. The breadcrumbs and almonds give the pizza topping an extra crunch.*

SERVES 2–4

2 tbsp Parmesan cheese, grated
1 quantity Potato Base (see page 12)
1 quantity Tomato Sauce (see page 15)
175 g/6 oz fresh spinach leaves
1 small red onion, sliced thinly
2 tbsp olive oil
¼ tsp freshly grated nutmeg
2 hard-boiled eggs
15 g/½ oz fresh white breadcrumbs
60 g/2 oz Jarlsberg cheese, grated (or
    Emmental, Cheddar or Gruyère, if not
    available)
2 tbsp flaked (slivered) almonds
olive oil for drizzling
salt and pepper

**1** Mix the Parmesan cheese with the potato base. Roll out or press the dough, using a rolling pin or your hands, into a 25 cm/10 in circle on a lightly floured work surface. Place on a large greased baking sheet or pizza pan and push up the edge slightly. Spread with the tomato sauce almost to the edge.

**2** Remove the stalks from the spinach and wash the leaves thoroughly in plenty of cold water. Drain the spinach well and pat off the excess water with paper towels.

**3** Fry the onion gently in the oil for 5 minutes until softened. Add the spinach and continue to fry until just wilted. Drain off any excess liquid produced. Place on the pizza and sprinkle over the nutmeg.

**4** Remove the shells from the eggs and slice. Arrange on the spinach.

**5** Mix together the breadcrumbs, cheese and almonds, and sprinkle over. Drizzle with a little olive oil and season well.

**6** Bake in a preheated oven at 200°C/400°F/Gas Mark 6 for 18–20 minutes, or until the edge is crisp and golden. Serve immediately.

### SPINACH

If fresh spinach is unavailable, use frozen whole leaf spinach. Spinach carries a lot of water so drain out as much as possible or you will end up with a soggy base.

STEP 1

STEP 2

STEP 3

STEP 6

# RATATOUILLE AND LENTIL

*The ultimate vegetarian pizza! Ratatouille and lentils on a wholemeal bread base are topped with vegetarian Cheddar cheese and sunflower seeds. You can use canned green lentils, which do not have to be soaked or cooked before being used; you will need about 125 g/4 oz.*

SERVES 2–4

60 g/2 oz green lentils
½ small aubergine (eggplant), diced
1 small onion, sliced
1 garlic clove, crushed
3 tbsp olive oil
½ courgette (zucchini), sliced
½ red (bell) pepper, sliced
½ green (bell) pepper, sliced
220 g/7½ oz can chopped tomatoes
1 tbsp chopped fresh oregano or 1 tsp dried
1 quantity Bread Dough Base made with
  wholemeal flour (see page 8)
60 g/2 oz vegetarian Cheddar cheese, sliced
  thinly
1 tbsp sunflower seeds
olive oil for drizzling
salt and pepper

**1** Soak the lentils in hot water for 30 minutes. Drain and rinse; then simmer in a pan covered with fresh water for 10 minutes.

**2** Sprinkle the aubergine (eggplant) with a little salt in a colander and allow the bitter juices to drain over a sink for about 20 minutes. Rinse and pat dry with paper towels.

**3** Fry the onion and garlic gently in the oil for 3 minutes. Add the courgette (zucchini), (bell) peppers and aubergine (eggplant). Cover and leave to 'sweat' over a low heat for about 5 minutes.

**4** Add the tomatoes, drained lentils, oregano, 2 tbsp water and seasoning. Cover and simmer for 15 minutes, stirring occasionally, adding more water if necessary.

**5** Roll out or press the dough, using a rolling pin or your hands, into a 25 cm/10 in circle on a lightly floured work surface. Place on a large greased baking sheet or pizza pan and push up the edge slightly. Cover and leave to rise slightly for 10 minutes in a warm place.

**6** Spread the ratatouille over the dough base almost to the edge. Arrange the cheese slices on top and sprinkle over the sunflower seeds. Drizzle with a little olive oil and season.

**7** Bake in a preheated oven at 200°C/400°F/Gas Mark 6 for 18–20 minutes, or until the edge is crisp and golden. Serve immediately.

# THREE CHEESE AND ARTICHOKE

*Sliced artichokes combined with Dolcelatte, Cheddar and Parmesan cheeses give a really delicious topping to this pizza. Artichoke hearts can be bought either canned or in jars in olive oil. If you use the ones in oil, you can use the oil to drizzle over the pizza before baking.*

STEP 1

SERVES 2–4

*1 quantity Bread Dough Base (see page 8)*
*1 quantity Special Tomato Sauce (see page 16)*
*60 g/2 oz Dolcelatte cheese, sliced*
*125 g/4 oz artichoke hearts in oil, sliced*
*½ small red onion, chopped*
*45 g/1½ oz Cheddar cheese, grated*
*2 tbsp Parmesan cheese, grated*
*1 tbsp chopped fresh thyme*
*oil from artichokes for drizzling*
*salt and pepper*

**1** Roll out or press the dough, using a rolling pin or your hands, into a 25 cm/10 in circle on a lightly floured work surface. Place the base on a large greased baking sheet or pizza pan and push up the edge slightly.

**2** Cover and leave to rise for 10 minutes in a warm place. Spread with the tomato sauce almost to the edge.

**3** Arrange the Dolcelatte cheese on the tomato sauce, followed by the artichoke hearts and red onion.

**4** Mix the Cheddar and Parmesan cheeses together with the thyme

STEP 3

and sprinkle the mixture over the pizza. Drizzle a little of the oil from the jar of artichokes over the pizza and season to taste.

**5** Bake in a preheated oven at 200°C/400°F/Gas Mark 6 for 18–20 minutes, or until the edge is crisp and golden and the cheese is bubbling.

**6** Serve immediately with a fresh salad of lettuce leaves and cherry tomato halves.

STEP 4

## CHEESES AND SALADS

You can use any cheese of your choice, as long as it complements the others. Remember that a strongly flavoured cheese will dominate the others. For the accompanying salad, buy a bag of mixed prepared lettuce leaves, as it saves buying several whole lettuces of different kinds.

STEP 6

**STEP 1**

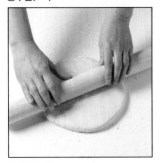

**STEP 2**

**STEP 3**

**STEP 4**

# GIARDINIERA

*As the name implies, this colourful pizza should be topped with fresh vegetables grown in the garden, but as many of us do not have space to grow anything more than a few flowers, we have to rely on other sources. The vegetables used here are only a suggestion; you can replace them with the same quantity of anything that is available.*

SERVES 2–4

6 fresh spinach leaves
1 quantity Potato Base (see page 12)
1 quantity Special Tomato Sauce (see page 16)
1 tomato, sliced
1 celery stick, sliced thinly
1/2 green (bell) pepper, sliced thinly
1 baby courgette (zucchini), sliced
30 g/1 oz asparagus tips
30 g/1 oz sweetcorn, defrosted if frozen
30 g/1 oz peas, defrosted if frozen
4 spring onions (scallions), trimmed and chopped
1 tbsp chopped fresh mixed herbs, such as tarragon and parsley
60 g/2 oz Mozzarella cheese, grated
2 tbsp Parmesan cheese, grated
1 artichoke heart
olive oil for drizzling
salt and pepper

**1** Remove any stalks from the spinach and wash the leaves in plenty of cold water. Pat dry with paper towels.

**2** Roll out or press the potato base, using a rolling pin or your hands, into a large 25 cm/10 in circle on a lightly floured work surface. Place the round on a large greased baking sheet or pizza pan and push up the edge a little to form a rim. Spread with the tomato sauce.

**3** Arrange the spinach leaves on the sauce, followed by the tomato slices. Top with the remaining vegetables and herbs.

**4** Mix together the cheeses and sprinkle over. Place the artichoke heart in the centre. Drizzle the pizza with a little olive oil and season.

**5** Bake in a preheated oven at 200°C/400°F/Gas Mark 6 for 18–20 minutes, or until the edges are crisp and golden. Serve immediately.

### SPINACH

Bags of young spinach leaves are available in most supermarkets. The spinach has been pre-washed and the large stalks have been removed. Use the required amount of spinach on the pizza and use the remainder in a salad.

STEP 2

STEP 3

STEP 3

STEP 4

# WILD MUSHROOM AND WALNUT

*Wild mushrooms make a delicious pizza topping when mixed with walnuts and Roquefort cheese. If possible, use a mixture of oyster and shiitake mushrooms and ceps.*

SERVES 2–4

*1 quantity Scone (Biscuit) Base (see page 10)*
*1 quantity Special Tomato Sauce (see page 16)*
*125 g/4 oz soft cheese*
*1 tbsp chopped fresh mixed herbs, such as parsley, oregano and basil*
*250 g/8 oz wild mushrooms, such as oyster, shiitake or ceps, or 125 g/4 oz each wild and button mushrooms*
*2 tbsp olive oil*
*¼ tsp fennel seeds*
*30 g/1 oz walnuts, roughly chopped*
*45 g/1½ oz Roquefort cheese*
*olive oil to drizzle*
*salt and pepper*
*sprig of flat-leaf (Italian) parsley to garnish*

**1** Roll out or press the scone (biscuit) base, using a rolling pin or your hands, into a 25 cm/10 in circle on a lightly floured work surface. Place on a large greased baking sheet or pizza pan and push up the edge a little with your fingers to form a rim.

**2** Spread with the tomato sauce almost to the edge. Dot with the soft cheese and herbs.

**3** Wipe and slice the mushrooms. Heat the oil in a large frying pan or wok and stir-fry the mushrooms and fennel seeds for 2–3 minutes. Spread over the pizza with the walnuts.

**4** Crumble the cheese over the pizza, drizzle with a little olive oil and season.

**5** Bake in a preheated oven at 200°C/400°F/Gas Mark 6 for 18–20 minutes, or until the edge is crisp and golden. Serve immediately garnished with a sprig of flat-leaf (Italian) parsley.

## MUSHROOMS

Wild mushrooms each have their own distinctive flavours and make a change from button mushrooms. But they can be very expensive, so you can always use a mixture with crimini or the more common button mushrooms instead.

## GARLIC FLAVOUR

For added flavour, use a soft cheese with garlic and herbs.

# ROASTED VEGETABLE AND GOAT'S CHEESE

*Wonderfully colourful vegetables are roasted in olive oil with thyme and garlic. The goat's cheese adds a nutty, piquant flavour.*

SERVES 2–4

2 baby courgettes (zucchini), halved
    lengthways
2 baby aubergines (eggplant), quartered
    lengthways
$^1/_2$ red (bell) pepper, cut into 4 strips
$^1/_2$ yellow (bell) pepper, cut into 4 strips
1 small red onion, cut into wedges
2 whole garlic cloves
4 tbsp olive oil
1 tbsp red wine vinegar
1 tbsp chopped fresh thyme
1 quantity Bread Dough Base (see page 8)
1 quantity Tomato Sauce (see page 15)
90 g/ 3 oz goat's cheese
salt and pepper
fresh basil leaves to garnish

**1** Place all the prepared vegetables in a large roasting tin. Mix together the olive oil, vinegar, thyme and plenty of seasoning and pour over, coating all the vegetables well.

**2** Bake in a preheated oven at 200°C/400°F/Gas Mark 6 for 15–20 minutes until the skins on the vegetables have started to blacken in places. Turn the vegetables over half-way through cooking. Leave the vegetables to rest for 5 minutes after roasting.

**3** Carefully peel off the skins from the roast (bell) peppers and the garlic cloves. Slice the garlic.

**4** Roll out or press the dough, using a rolling pin or your hands, into a 25 cm/10 in circle on a lightly floured work surface. Place on a large greased baking sheet or pizza pan and raise the edge a little. Cover and leave for 10 minutes to rise slightly in a warm place. Spread with the tomato sauce almost to the edge.

**5** Arrange the roasted vegetables on top and dot with the cheese. Drizzle the oil and juices from the roasting tin over the pizza and season.

**6** Bake in a preheated oven at 200°C/400°F/Gas Mark 6 for 18–20 minutes, or until the edge is crisp and golden. Serve immediately garnished with basil leaves.

### SUBSTITUTES

If baby courgettes (zucchini) and aubergines (eggplants) are unavailable, use a small sliced courgette (zucchini) and quarter slices of half a small aubergine (eggplant).

STEP 1

STEP 2

STEP 3

STEP 4

# TOFU CHINESE-STYLE

*Chunks of tofu marinated in ginger and soy sauce impart something of an oriental flavour to this pizza. The base is made from semolina, which gives it an unusual texture.*

SERVES 2–4

*1 litre/1 ³/₄ pints milk*
*1 tsp salt*
*250 g/8 oz semolina*
*1 tbsp soy sauce*
*1 tbsp dry sherry*
*¹/₂ tsp fresh grated ginger root*
*285 g/9¹/₂ oz pack tofu, cut into chunks*
*2 eggs*
*60 g/2 oz Parmesan cheese, grated*
*1 quantity Tomato Sauce (see page 15)*
*30 g/1 oz baby sweetcorn, cut into 4*
*30 g/1 oz mangetout (snow peas), trimmed and cut into 4*
*4 spring onions (scallions), trimmed and cut into 2.5 cm/1 in strips*
*60 g/2 oz Mozzarella cheese, sliced thinly*
*2 tsp sesame oil*
*salt and pepper*

**1** Bring the milk to the boil with the salt. Sprinkle the semolina over the surface, stirring all the time. Cook for 10 minutes over a low heat, stirring occasionally, taking care not to let it burn. Remove from the heat and leave to cool until tepid.

**2** Mix the soy sauce, sherry and ginger together in a bowl, add the tofu and stir gently to coat. Leave to marinate in a cool place for about 20 minutes.

**3** Beat the eggs with a little pepper. Add to the semolina with the Parmesan cheese and mix well. Place on a large greased baking sheet or in a pizza pan and pat into a 25 cm/10 in round, using the back of a metal spoon or wetted hands. Spread with the tomato sauce almost to the edge.

**4** Blanch the sweetcorn and mangetout (snow peas) in boiling water for 1 minute, drain and place on the pizza with the drained tofu. Top with the spring onions (scallions) and slices of cheese. Drizzle over the sesame oil and season.

**5** Bake in a preheated oven at 200°C/400°F/Gas Mark 6 for 18–20 minutes, or until the edge is crisp and golden. Serve immediately.

## GINGER

Ginger root freezes well, so keep some in the freezer and just break off pieces when required. Ginger root should be peeled before grating or chopping.

# CHAPTER FOUR

# *Different Pizza Shapes*

We usually think of a pizza as being round, but pizzas can be made in many shapes and sizes. Often they are made in a rectangle and cut into squares or strips to serve.

If you use alternative bases to the more traditional doughs, you will get a variety of different shapes depending on what you use. For instance, French bread pizzas are long and narrow, as the bases are made from a French loaf that has been halved lengthways. These make very good pizza bases, particularly as they are quick to prepare, and make perfect individual meals.

Pitta (pocket) breads, muffins, rolls, baps and croissants can all be used for bases. As they have all been pre-cooked, care must be taken not to overbake them, as this will result in a dried-out base. In some cases it might be preferable to cook the pizza under a grill (broiler) rather than bake it, as this would cook the topping without drying out the base.

Opposite: *The Spanish Steps in the city of Rome, covered as always with a stunning floral display.*

STEP 1

STEP 2

STEP 3

STEP 4

# PISSALADIERE

*This is a traditional French Provençal pizza, in which the main ingredient is onions. A lattice pattern is made with anchovies and black olives. This pizza is rectangular in shape and can be cut into squares or strips to serve.*

MAKES 6 SQUARES

*4 tbsp olive oil*
*3 onions, sliced thinly*
*1 garlic clove, crushed*
*1tsp soft brown sugar*
*¹/₂ tsp crushed fresh rosemary*
*220 g/7¹/₂ oz can chopped tomatoes*
*1 quantity Bread Dough Base (see page 8)*
*2 tbsp grated Parmesan cheese*
*60 g/2 oz can anchovies*
*12–14 black olives*
*salt and black pepper*

**1** Heat 3 tbsp of the oil in a large saucepan and add the onions, garlic, sugar and rosemary. Cover the pan and fry gently for 10 minutes until the onions have softened but not browned, stirring occasionally. Add the tomatoes, stir and season well. Leave to cool slightly.

**2** Roll out or press the dough, using a rolling pin or your hands, on a lightly floured work surface to fit a 30 x 18 cm/12 x 7 in greased Swiss roll tin. Place in the tin and push up the edges slightly.

**3** Brush the remaining oil over the dough and sprinkle with the cheese. Cover and leave to rise slightly in a warm place for about 10 minutes.

**4** Spread the onion and tomato topping over the base. Remove the anchovies from the can, reserving the oil. Split each anchovy in half lengthways and arrange on the pizza in a lattice pattern. Place olives in between the anchovies and drizzle over a little of the reserved oil. Season.

**5** Bake in a preheated oven at 200°C/400°F/Gas Mark 6 for 18–20 minutes, or until the edges are crisp and golden. Cut into squares and serve immediately.

PARTY PIZZA

For a great party pizza, make twice the size in a large greased roasting tin, doubling up on the ingredients, and bake until the edges are golden.

STEP 1

STEP 2

STEP 3

STEP 5

# HAWAIIAN MUFFINS

*Halved toasted muffins are topped with pineapple and prosciutto, which is an Italian dry-cured ham. Plain, wholemeal or cheese muffins will all make great pizza bases.*

SERVES 4

*4 muffins*
*1 quantity Tomato Sauce (see page 15)*
*2 sun-dried tomatoes in oil, chopped*
*60 g/2 oz prosciutto ham*
*2 rings canned pineapple, chopped*
*¹/₂ green (bell) pepper, chopped*
*125 g/4 oz Mozzarella cheese, sliced thinly*
*olive oil for drizzling*
*salt and pepper*
*small fresh basil leaves to garnish*

**1** Cut the muffins in half and toast the cut side lightly.

**2** Divide the sauce evenly between the muffins and spread over.

**3** Sprinkle over the sun-dried tomatoes.

**4** Cut the ham into thin strips and place on the muffins with the pineapple and green (bell) pepper.

**5** Lay the Mozzarella slices on top.

**6** Drizzle a little olive oil over each pizza, and season.

**7** Place under a preheated medium grill and cook until the cheese melts and bubbles.

**8** Serve immediately garnished with small basil leaves.

### MUFFINS

You don't have to use plain muffins for your base; wholemeal or cheese muffins will also make ideal pizza bases. Muffins freeze well, so always keep some in the freezer for an instant pizza.

### PREPARING PINEAPPLE

To prepare a fresh pineapple, slice off the skin from the top, bottom and sides. Remove the eyes with a sharp knife or the end of a potato peeler. Cut the pineapple into chunks. The pineapple will lose a lot of juice as you peel it – save as much as you can, and drink it later.

# FRENCH BREAD PIZZAS

*Halved baguettes are a ready-made pizza base. The colours of the tomatoes and cheese contrast beautifully on top. Try an onion or a granary baguette, or Italian ciabatta bread, which makes a really good base.*

STEP 2

SERVES 4

2 baguettes
1 quantity Tomato Sauce (see page 15)
4 plum tomatoes, sliced thinly lengthways
150 g / 5 oz Mozzarella cheese, sliced thinly
10 black olives, cut into rings
8 fresh basil leaves, shredded
olive oil for drizzling
salt and pepper

**1** Cut the baguettes in half lengthways and toast the cut side of the bread lightly.

**2** Spread the toasted baguettes with the tomato sauce.

**3** Arrange the tomato and Mozzarella cheese slices alternately along the length.

**4** Top with the olive rings and half the basil. Drizzle over a little olive oil and season well.

**5** Either place under a preheated medium grill (broiler) and cook until the cheese melts and is bubbling or bake in a preheated oven at 200°C/400°F/Gas Mark 6 for 15–20 minutes.

**6** Sprinkle over the remaining basil and serve immediately.

STEP 3

## DIFFERENT BREAD BASES

There are many different types of bread available which would be suitable for these pizzas. Italian ciabatta bread is made with olive oil and is available both plain and with different ingredients, such as small pieces of black olives or sun-dried tomatoes, mixed in.

STEP 4

## INSTANT PIZZA

Make up double quantities and freeze half of the pizzas. Reheat them from frozen in the oven for about 15 minutes for an instant snack.

STEP 6

STEP 2

STEP 3

STEP 4

STEP 5

# CALZONE

*A calzone is like a pizza in reverse – it resembles a large pasty with the dough on the outside and the filling on the inside. In Italian the word 'calzone' actually means trousers! If you are going on a picnic, take a calzone pizza as it can be eaten cold and is easy to transport.*

SERVES 2–4

*1 quantity Bread Dough Base (see page 8)*
*1 egg, beaten*
*1 tomato*
*1 tbsp tomato purée*
*30 g/1 oz Italian salami, chopped*
*30 g/1 oz mortadella ham, chopped*
*30 g/1 oz Ricotta cheese*
*2 spring onions (scallions), trimmed and chopped*
*¼ tsp dried oregano*
*salt and pepper*

**1** Roll out the dough into a 23 cm/ 9 in circle on a lightly floured work surface.

**2** Brush the edge of the dough with a little beaten egg.

**3** To skin the tomato, cut a cross in the skin and immerse it in boiling water for 45 seconds. Remove and rinse in cold water; the skin should slide off easily. Chop the tomato.

**4** Spread the tomato purée over half the circle nearest to you. Scatter the salami, mortadella and chopped tomato on top. Dot with the Ricotta cheese and sprinkle over the spring onions (scallions) and oregano. Season well.

**5** Fold over the other half of the dough to form a half moon. Press the edges together well to prevent the filling from coming out.

**6** Place on a baking sheet and brush with beaten egg to glaze. Make a hole in the top to allow steam to escape.

**7** Bake in a preheated oven at 200°C/400°F/Gas Mark 6 for 20 minutes, or until golden.

VEGETARIAN VERSION

For a vegetarian calzone, replace the salami and mortadella with mushrooms or cooked chopped spinach.

STEP 1

STEP 4

STEP 6

STEP 7

# CALIFORNIAN

*The vibrant colours of the (bell) peppers and onion make this a delightful pizza. Served cut into fingers, it is ideal for a party or buffet.*

MAKES 8

1 quantity Bread Dough Base (see page 8)
2 tbsp olive oil
¹/₂ each red, green and yellow (bell) pepper, sliced thinly
1 small red onion, sliced thinly
1 garlic clove, crushed
1 quantity Tomato Sauce (see page 15)
3 tbsp raisins
30 g/ 1 oz pine kernels
1 tbsp chopped fresh thyme
olive oil for drizzling
salt and pepper

**1** Roll out or press the dough, using a rolling pin or your hands, on a lightly floured work surface to fit a 30 x 18 cm/12 x 7 in greased Swiss roll tin.

**2** Place in the tin and push up the edges slightly.

**3** Cover and leave to rise slightly in a warm place for about 10 minutes.

**4** Heat the oil in a large frying pan. Add the (bell) peppers, onion and garlic, and fry gently for 5 minutes until they have softened but not browned. Leave to cool.

**5** Spread the tomato sauce over the base almost to the edge.

**6** Sprinkle over the raisins and top with the cooled (bell) pepper mixture. Add the pine kernels and thyme. Drizzle with a little olive oil and season well.

**7** Bake in a preheated oven at 200°C/400°F/Gas Mark 6 for 18–20 minutes, or until the edges are crisp and golden. Cut into fingers and serve immediately.

## RAISINS

Soak the raisins in some warm water for 15 minutes before adding them to the pizza, as this will keep them plump and moist when they are baked.

STEP 1

STEP 4

STEP 5

STEP 6

# MINI PITTA BREAD CANAPES

*Smoked salmon and asparagus make extra special party pizza canapés.*
*Mini pitta breads make great bases and are really quick.*

MAKES 16

*8 thin asparagus spears*
*16 mini pitta breads*
*1 quantity Special Tomato Sauce (see page 16)*
*30 g/1 oz mild Cheddar cheese, grated*
*30 g/1 oz Ricotta cheese*
*60 g/2 oz smoked salmon*
*olive oil for drizzling*
*pepper*

**1** Cut the asparagus spears into 2.5 cm/1 in lengths; then cut each piece in half lengthways.

**2** Blanch the asparagus in boiling water for 1 minute. Drain and plunge into cold water.

**3** Place the pitta breads on 2 baking sheets. Spread about 1 tsp tomato sauce on each.

**4** Mix the cheeses together and divide between the 16 pitta breads.

**5** Cut the smoked salmon into 16 long thin strips. Arrange one strip on each pitta bread with the asparagus spears.

**6** Drizzle over a little olive oil and season with pepper.

**7** Bake in a preheated oven at 200°C/400°F/Gas Mark 6 for 8–10 minutes. Serve immediately.

## ECONOMY VERSIONS

Smoked salmon is expensive, so for a cheaper version, try using smoked trout. It is often half the price of smoked salmon, and tastes just as good. Try experimenting with other smoked fish, such as smoked mackerel, with its strong, distinctive flavour, for a bit of variety.

## ASPARAGUS

Blanching the asparagus helps to soften it before topping the canapes. Plunge it into cold water after blanching, as this helps it to keep its colour.

# CHAPTER FIVE

# *Inventive Pizzas*

In this section anything goes! Pizzas can be topped with almost any ingredient, so let your imagination go and make up your own individual recipes.

Pizza-making can be really fun for children. Let them create animal or funny faces from a range of ingredients such as vegetables, cheese and pasta. The results may help to encourage difficult eaters to clear their plates.

The Sunday morning fry-up will never be the same after trying a breakfast pizza – or even a corned beef hash pizza, which would be just as good for breakfast. Experiment with different flavours and you will be surprised by what you can come up with.

Opposite: *Rome's famous Trevi Fountain.*

**STEP 1**

**STEP 4**

**STEP 6**

**STEP 7**

# FUNNY FACES

*These individual pizzas have faces made from sliced vegetables and spaghetti or noodles. Children love pizzas and will enjoy making their own. Use whatever suitable vegetables you have and let them have fun making all sorts of funny faces.*

SERVES 4

*1 quantity Bread Dough Base (see page 8)*
*30 g / 1 oz spaghetti or egg noodles*
*1 quantity Tomato Sauce (see page 15)*
*8 slices pepperoni-style sausage*
*8 thin slices celery*
*4 slices button mushrooms*
*4 slices yellow (bell) pepper*
*4 slices Mozzarella cheese*
*4 slices courgette (zucchini)*
*olive oil for drizzling*
*8 peas*

**1** Divide the dough into 4. Roll each piece out into a 12 cm / 5 in diameter circle and place on greased baking sheets. Cover and leave to rise slightly in a warm place for about 10 minutes.

**2** Cook the spaghetti or egg noodles according to the packet instructions.

**3** Divide the tomato sauce evenly between each pizza base and spread out almost to the edge.

**4** To make the faces, use pepperoni slices for the main part of the eyes, celery for the eyebrows, mushrooms for

the noses and (bell) pepper slices for the mouths.

**5** Cut the Mozzarella cheese and courgette (zucchini) slices in half. Use the cheese for the cheeks and the courgettes (zucchini) for the ears.

**6** Drizzle a little olive oil over each pizza and bake in a preheated oven at 200°C/400°F/Gas Mark 6 for 12–15 minutes until the edges are crisp and golden.

**7** Transfer the pizzas to serving plates and place the peas in the centre of the eyes. Drain the spaghetti or noodles and arrange around the tops of the pizzas for hair. Serve immediately.

### CAT PIZZA

Make cat-face pizzas by using chicory for the ears, a mushroom for the nose and spaghetti for whiskers. Cut out cat eye shapes from pepperoni or (bell) peppers, and add a pasta bow tie.

STEP 2

STEP 3

STEP 4

STEP 6

# BREAKFAST

*For a really substantial start to the morning, try a breakfast pizza!
Sausages, bacon and mushrooms on a bread base topped with a fried egg
will probably see you through the day.*

SERVES 4

*1 quantity Bread Dough Base (see page 8)*
*12 skinless cocktail sausages*
*3 tbsp oil*
*1 quantity Tomato Sauce (see page 15)*
*150 g / 5 oz can baked beans*
*4 rashers back bacon*
*60 g / 2 oz baby button mushrooms, wiped*
  *and quartered*
*1 small tomato, cut into 8 wedges*
*60 g / 2 oz Cheddar cheese, grated*
*4 eggs*
*salt and pepper*

**1** Roll out or press the dough, using a rolling pin or your hands, into a 25 cm / 10 in circle on a lightly floured work surface. Place on a large greased baking sheet or pizza pan and push up the edge slightly to form a rim. Cover and leave to rise slightly for 10 minutes in a warm place.

**2** Brown the sausages in a frying pan with 1 tbsp of the oil.

**3** Mix the tomato sauce with the baked beans and spread over the base almost to the edge. Add the sausages on top.

**4** Cut the bacon into strips and arrange on the pizza with the mushrooms and tomato. Sprinkle over the cheese and season.

**5** Bake in a preheated oven at 200°C/400°F/Gas Mark 6 for 18–20 minutes, or until the edge is crisp and golden.

**6** Add the remaining oil to the frying pan and fry the eggs. When the pizza is cooked, cut into 4 and top each with a fried egg. Serve immediately.

### PLANNING AHEAD

To save time in the morning, you can make the tomato sauce and bread dough the night before. After the dough has been kneaded, wrap well and place in the refrigerator (if it is cold enough, this should prevent the dough from rising). After rolling out, the dough will take about 10 minutes longer to rise.

STEP 1

STEP 2

STEP 3

STEP 4

# CORNED BEEF HASH

*A combination of corned beef and baked eggs on a soured cream and potato base makes a really unusual pizza. Make sure each well is big enough to hold an egg before dropping it in!*

SERVES 2–4

*500 g/1 lb potatoes*
*3 tbsp soured cream*
*325 g/11 oz can corned beef*
*1 small onion, chopped finely*
*1 green (bell) pepper, chopped*
*3 tbsp tomato and chilli relish*
*1 quantity Special Tomato Sauce (see page 16)*
*4 eggs*
*30 g/1 oz Mozzarella cheese, grated*
*30 g/1 oz Cheddar cheese, grated*
*paprika*
*salt and pepper*
*chopped fresh parsley to garnish*

**1** Peel the potatoes and cut into even-sized chunks. Parboil them for 5 minutes in boiling salted water. Drain, rinse in cold water and cool.

**2** Grate the potatoes and mix with the soured cream and seasoning in a bowl. Place on a large greased baking sheet or pizza pan and pat out into a 25 cm/10 in circle, pushing up the edge slightly to form a rim.

**3** Mash the corned beef roughly with a fork and stir in the onion, green (bell) pepper and relish. Season well.

**4** Spread the tomato sauce over the potato base almost to the edge. Top with the corned beef mixture. Using a spoon, make 4 wells in the corned beef. Break an egg into each.

**5** Mix the cheeses together and sprinkle over the pizza with a little paprika. Season well.

**6** Bake in a preheated oven at 200°C/400°F/Gas Mark 6 for 20–25 minutes until the eggs have cooked but still have slightly runny yolks. Serve immediately garnished with chopped parsley.

### ADDED EXTRAS

For extra colour, mix a grated carrot with the potato base. This will look and taste good, and will help to persuade your children to eat their vegetables, if they are fussy about that sort of thing. Use the tomato and chilli relish sparingly if you are serving this to children.

# SPICY MEATBALL

*Small minced (ground) beef meatballs, spiced with chillies and cumin seeds and covered in cheese and bacon, are baked on a scone (biscuit) base.*

STEP 1

SERVES 2–4

250 g/8 oz lean minced (ground) beef
30 g/1 oz jalapeño chillies in brine, chopped
1 tsp cumin seeds
1 tbsp chopped fresh parsley
1 tbsp beaten egg
3 tbsp olive oil
1 quantity Scone (Biscuit) Base (see page 10)
1 quantity Tomato Sauce (see page 15)
30 g/1 oz pimiento, sliced
2 rashers streaky bacon, cut into strips
60 g/2 oz Cheddar cheese, grated
olive oil for drizzling
salt and pepper
chopped fresh parsley to garnish

**1** Mix the beef, chillies, cumin seeds, parsley and egg together in a bowl and season. Form into 12 small meatballs. Cover and chill for 1 hour.

**2** Heat the oil in a large frying pan. Add the meatballs and brown all over. Remove with a perforated spoon or fish slice and drain on paper towels.

**3** Roll out or press the dough, using a rolling pin or your hands, into a 25 cm/10 in circle on a lightly floured work surface. Place on a greased baking sheet or pizza pan and push up the edge slightly to form a rim. Spread with the tomato sauce almost to the edge.

STEP 2

**4** Arrange the meatballs on the pizza with the pimiento and bacon. Sprinkle over the cheese and drizzle with a little olive oil. Season.

**5** Bake in a preheated oven at 200°C/400°F/Gas Mark 6 for 18–20 minutes, or until the edge is golden and crisp.

**6** Serve immediately garnished with chopped parsley.

STEP 3

### MEATBALLS

If time allows, make the meatballs and chill them for an hour before frying as this will help to stop them from breaking up during cooking.

STEP 4

STEP 1

STEP 3

STEP 5

STEP 8

# AVOCADO AND HAM

*A smoked ham and avocado salad is served on a pizza with a base enriched with chopped sun-dried tomatoes and black olives, which are kneaded into the dough. If you are unable to buy Pipo Crème cheese, use blue Brie instead.*

SERVES 2–4

1 quantity Bread Dough Base (see page 8)
4 sun-dried tomatoes, chopped
30 g/ 1 oz black olives, chopped
1 quantity Special Tomato Sauce (see page 16)
4 small chicory (endive) leaves, shredded
4 small radicchio lettuce leaves, shredded
1 avocado, peeled, pitted and sliced
60 g/ 2 oz wafer-thin smoked ham
60 g/ 2 oz Pipo Crème or other blue cheese, cut into small pieces
olive oil for drizzling
salt and pepper
chopped fresh chervil to garnish

**1** Knead the dough gently, adding the sun-dried tomatoes and olives until mixed in.

**2** Roll out or press the dough, using a rolling pin or your hands, into a 25 cm/ 10 in circle on a lightly floured work surface. Place on a greased baking sheet or pizza pan and push up the edge a little to form a rim.

**3** Cover and leave to rise slightly in a warm place for 10 minutes before spreading with tomato sauce almost to the edge.

**4** Top the pizza with shredded lettuce leaves and avocado slices.

**5** Scrunch up the ham and add with the cheese.

**6** Drizzle with a little olive oil and season well.

**7** Bake in a preheated oven at 200°C/400°F/Gas Mark 6 for 18–20 minutes, or until the edge is crisp and golden.

**8** Sprinkle with chervil to garnish and serve immediately.

### HELPFUL HINTS

Before you use them, toss the avocado slices in a little fresh lemon juice to prevent the flesh from turning too brown. For a change, you could use wafer-thin smoked turkey instead of ham.

# MAKING PIZZAS

## TIPS

**Pizza bases and their ingredients**

Buy fresh yeast in bulk and freeze in 15g/$^1$/$_2$ oz quantities ready to use whenever needed.

To give the base extra flavour and a different texture, try adding to the flour fresh or dried herbs, chopped nuts or seeds, such as poppy, sunflower and sesame.

Always use a good olive oil such as extra virgin for the best flavour.

If time is short, place the bread dough in a food processor for a few minutes to knead.

If you have made the bread dough or scone (biscuit) base too wet, add a little extra flour and work it in. If the base is too dry, add a little extra water or milk in the same way.

Bread dough bases can be kept for several days before being used. After kneading, carefully wrap in clingfilm (plastic wrap) to prevent them from drying out in the refrigerator. Allow extra time for the dough to rise, as it will take a while for the dough to warm up and for the yeast to begin to work.

If the dough is left uncovered and develops a crust, cover it with a damp cloth and the crust will soon disappear.

## THE HISTORY OF THE PIZZA

The pizza has become a universally popular food, in every form from the genuine article – thin, crisp and oven-baked – to frozen and fast-food pizza slices. The delightful aroma of freshly baked bread topped with tomatoes, fresh herbs and cheese rarely fails to have a mouthwatering effect. As well as being economical and popular, few other dishes are so versatile, thanks to the countless possible permutations of bases and toppings that can be served to suit every palate.

Although there is much speculation about where pizza in its simplest form was first invented, it is usually associated with the old Italian town of Naples. It was then a simple street food, richly flavoured and quickly made. It was not always round and flat as we know it today, but was originally folded up like a book, with the filling inside, and eaten by hand. Pizzas were usually sold on the streets by street criers who carried them around in copper cylindrical drums kept hot by coals from the pizza ovens.

The word pizza actually means any kind of pie. The classic Napoletana pizza is probably the best-known of the many varieties. This consists of a thin crust of dough topped simply with a fresh tomato sauce, Mozzarella cheese, olives, anchovies and a sprinkling of oregano. When baked, the flavours blend perfectly together to give the distinctive aromatic pizza. Another classic is the 'Margherita'

pizza, named after the Italian Queen Margherita. Bored with their usual cuisine when on a visit to Naples, she asked to sample a local speciality. The local 'Pizzaiolo' created a pizza in the colours of the Italian flag – red tomatoes, green basil and white Mozzarella. The Queen was delighted, and it became widely celebrated.

## THE BASIC INGREDIENTS

Pizzas are made from very basic ingredients and are very simple to cook. Although making your own base and topping can be a little time-consuming, it is very straightforward, and you end up with a delicious home-baked dish, as well as a sense of achievement.

**Flour**

Traditional pizza bases are made from bread dough, which is usually made with strong plain bread flour. However, for the best results use ordinary plain flour. A strong flour will make the dough very difficult to stretch into whatever shape you choose to make your pizza. For a brown bread base, use one of the many types of wholemeal flours available on the market, such as stoneground wholemeal, wheatmeal and granary. Wheatgerm or bran can also be added to white flour for extra flavour, fibre and interest. Or you could mix equal quantities of wholemeal and white flour. Always sift the flour first, as this will remove any lumps and help to incorporate air, which will in turn help to produce a light dough. If you sift wholemeal flours, there will be some bran, etc. left in the sieve which is normally tipped back into the sifted flour so as to benefit from it.

Yeast thrives in warm surroundings, so all the ingredients for the bread dough base should be warm, as should the equipment used. If the yeast is added to a cold bowl containing cold flour, the tepid yeast liquid will quickly cool down and this will retard its growth, and the dough will take much longer to rise. If the flour is kept in a cool cupboard or larder, remember to get it out in plenty of time to allow it to warm to room temperature before you use it. Sift the flour into a large mixing bowl, then place it somewhere warm, such as an airing cupboard or even in a top oven on the lowest setting. Do not allow it to overheat, as this will kill the yeast.

## Salt
Add the required amount of salt to the flour when sifting, as this will help to distribute it evenly. Salt is important, as it helps to develop the gluten in the flour. Gluten is the protein which produces the elasticity of the dough, but mostly it gives the dough its flavour.

## Yeast
There are three types of yeast available: fresh, dried and easy-blend. Fresh is usually found in health-food shops and is not expensive. Dissolve 15g/$^1$/$_2$ oz fresh yeast in 90ml/3$^1$/$_2$ fl oz tepid water with 2.5ml/$^1$/$_2$ tsp sugar and allow it to froth before adding it to the flour – about 5

minutes. The frothiness indicates that the yeast is working. Fresh yeast will keep for 4 to 5 days in the refrigerator. Make sure it is well covered, as it will dry out very quickly.

Dried yeast can be found in sachets or drums in most supermarkets and chemists. It has a shelf life of about 6 months, so buy only a small drum if you are not going to make bread dough on a regular basis. It is easy to make up a dough that won't rise, only to find out too late that the yeast has passed the sell-by date. Like fresh yeast, add it to the tepid water with a little sugar, and stir to dissolve. Allow the mixture to stand for 10-15 minutes until froth develops on the surface.

Easy-blend yeast is the simplest to use, as it is simply stirred dry into the flour before the water is added. It is available in sachet form and can be found in most supermarkets.

## Water
It has been said that Naples produces the best pizzas because of the quality of its water! But as that may be a bit far to travel just to make a pizza, your local water will suffice. The water must be tepid, as this is the optimum temperature for the yeast to grow. Take care to add just the right amount of water stated in the recipe. If you add too much water, the dough will be difficult to handle and the cooked base will be too hard.

## Kneading
This can be the most daunting procedure in bread-making but is a very necessary one. The best way of doing it is to take

### Fillings and toppings
Avoid using starchy topping ingredients, as the base is very substantial and you will end up with a heavy pizza.

Make sure that you season the tomato sauce well, as this is the basis of the pizza, and a bland sauce will make for a bland pizza. Using a bay leaf makes a considerable difference – but don't forget to take it out!

Do not overfill a pizza, as it will overflow in the oven and will be difficult to eat.

Make a rim around the edge of the dough, as this will help to keep the topping on.

When making pizza for several people with differing tastes, place different toppings on separate sections of the pizza, or make individual ones in a selection of flavours. They can all cook at the same time, making it easy to suit all tastes.

To make pizza easier to handle, put the heavier topping ingredients near the edge of the pizza rather than in the middle. This will help to prevent it from sagging at the point when cut into wedges.

Drain all the pizza ingredients as much as possible before they are used. If you use spinach, squeeze out as much water as possible, or you will end up with a soggy pizza.

Grease the pizza pan or baking sheet well, to prevent the pizza from sticking.

### Serving
Always serve a pizza as soon as it leaves the oven, as the cheese will set slightly and lose its elasticity as it cools down.

Place the pizza on a warmed serving plate when it comes out of the oven, to prevent it from going cold too quickly. Use a couple of large fish slices to transfer the pizza from the baking sheet or pizza pan to the serving plate.

Pizzas make excellent party food. Make them in large rectangles and cut into squares to serve.

### Leftovers
Any leftover Mozzarella cheese can be grated and frozen, ready for the next time you want to make a pizza.

Leftover tomato sauce can be used up by adding it to casseroles, soups, and pasta dish sauces such as spaghetti and lasagne.

### Accompaniments
Follow a pizza meal with a refreshing dessert, such as fresh fruit salad, sorbet or ice cream. Zabaglione, a light Italian dessert of eggs, sugar and Marsala wine, makes a perfect ending.

the edge of the dough that is furthest away from you and pull it into the centre towards you, then push it down with the heel of your hand, turning the dough round with your other hand as you go. The kneading process mixes all the ingredients together and strengthens the gluten, which holds the bubbles of air created by the yeast, which in turn causes the dough to rise. The dough must be kneaded for at least 5 minutes or until it becomes smooth and pliable and is no longer sticky.

Try adding extra ingredients to the dough when kneading, such as chopped sun-dried tomatoes or olives to create a more interesting base.

### The tomato sauce
Every pizza must have tomato sauce of some kind as the basis of the topping. This can be made using either canned or fresh tomatoes. There are many types of canned tomato available – for example, plum tomatoes, or tomatoes chopped in water, or chopped sieved tomato (passata). The chopped variety are often canned with added flavours such as garlic, basil, onion, chilli and mixed herbs, which will add more interest to your sauce. Make sure the sauce is well seasoned before adding it to your base, as a tasteless sauce will spoil your pizza.

### Cheese
The cheese most often associated with the pizza is, of course, Mozzarella. It is a mild, white, delicate cheese traditionally made from buffalo milk. The best feature of this cheese as far as pizzas are concerned is its ability to melt and

produce strings of cheese when a slice is cut and pulled away. It is sold in supermarkets, wrapped in small bags of whey to keep it moist. Slice, grate or cut it into small pieces before placing it on the pizza. Many supermarkets stock bags of pre-grated Mozzarella cheese, which is a great timesaver.

The other cheeses most often found on pizzas are Parmesan and Cheddar. The recipes in this book use a variety of different cheeses. If you are using strongly flavoured topping ingredients such as anchovies and olives, a milder-tasting cheese may be more suitable. Experiment with different cheeses to suit your taste.

### TOPPING INGREDIENTS

There are a number of classic ingredients that are used regularly in pizza toppings, such as olives, anchovies, capers, mushrooms, (bell) peppers, artichokes and chillies, but most ingredients are suitable, if used in complementary combinations. Be adventurous and experiment, but don't be afraid to stick to simple combinations of just two or three ingredients – often the simplest pizzas are the most delicious and the most memorable, as the flavours don't fight each other.

### Herbs
Whenever possible, use fresh herbs. They are becoming more readily available, especially since the introduction of 'growing' herbs, small pots of herbs which you buy from the supermarket or greengrocer and grow at home. This not

only ensures the herbs are as fresh as possible, but also provides a continuous supply.

If you use dried herbs, remember that you need only about one third of dried to fresh. The most popular pizza herbs are basil, oregano and parsley, although you can experiment with your favourite ones. Torn leaves of fresh basil on a tomato base is a simple but deliciously aromatic combination.

## Baking

Traditionally pizzas are cooked in special ovens on a stone hearth. A large peel or paddle is used to slide them in and out. But at home it is best to place the dough on a baking sheet or in a pizza pan. The dough will expand while cooking, so make sure the baking sheet is big enough. Always push up the edge of the dough to form a rim to prevent the topping from spilling over while it cooks.

## Time-savers

Fortunately for the busy cook, pizzas are an easy food to package and chill or freeze, ready to be cooked on demand. There is a wide range of ready-made pizza bases, either in packet form which only need to be mixed and shaped before they are ready for a topping, which can also be bought separately, most often in jars.

Pizzas are also sold complete with a variety of toppings, which you can bake as they are, or add more toppings yourself. Although they never seem to taste as good as a real homemade pizza, they can be very useful to keep on hand. Jars of peppers, sun-dried tomatoes and

artichokes in olive oil make very good toppings, and will keep for quite a while in your larder.

## Serving

Pizzas should be served as soon as they leave the oven. Cut the pizza into wedges or strips using a sharp knife or pizza cutter. As pizza slices are easy to eat by hand, they make great party food.

Crisp salads, coleslaw and garlic bread go well with pizzas and help to make a balanced meal. Due to their rich flavour pizzas are best served with a well-chilled Italian table wine such as Frascati, Valpolicella or Chianti. If you are not a wine drinker, beer will go with pizza just as well.

## Freezing

Pizzas are ideal standby food, as you can make and freeze them in advance, and both the bread dough and the complete pizza can be frozen. Make up double quantities of dough and freeze the half that is unused after it has been kneaded. Wrap in clingfilm (plastic wrap) and place in a freezer bag. Defrost at room temperature and allow to rise as normal. Alternatively, rise and roll out the dough, top with tomato sauce, cheese and any other topping ingredients and bake for only 10 minutes. Cool, wrap in a polythene bag and place in the freezer. Cook straight from the freezer in a hot oven for about 15 minutes.

The tomato sauce will keep well in a screw-topped jar in the refrigerator for up to a week, or can be placed in freezer-proof containers and frozen if you need to keep it for longer periods.

Garlic bread is often served with pizza. Mix 1–2 cloves of crushed garlic with 125g/4 oz butter and spread it in between diagonal cuts made in a French bread stick. Wrap in foil and place in the bottom of the oven for 5 or 6 minutes while the pizza is cooking.

For herb bread, add chopped fresh parsley and chives to the butter before spreading it on the bread.

## Salads

Salad-making has never been so simple, thanks to the bags of prepared salads available in most supermarkets. Choose a selection of unusual and exotic salad leaves to add colour and crunch to your salad. Chicory (endive), radiccio, oakleaf, curly endive, sorrel and lamb's lettuce all make an interesting change from the lettuce we are used to seeing in salads.

Use plenty of colour – red and yellow (bell) peppers, green mangetout (snow peas), cherry tomatoes and baby corn cobs are all readily available.

Make up your own dressing with 3 tbsp olive oil, 1 tbsp wholegrain mustard, 1 tbsp fresh chopped herbs and plenty of salt and pepper. Place in a screw-topped jar and shake well to blend. Pour over the prepared salad and toss well to mix. Add the dressing just before serving, or the lettuce leaves will wilt and go soggy.

# INDEX